Roxy the Raccoon

First published in 2018
by Jessica Kingsley Publishers
73 Collier Street
London N1 9BE, UK
and
400 Market Street, Suite 400
Philadelphia, PA 19106, USA

www.jkp.com

Library of Congress Cataloging in Publication Data
A CIP catalog record for this book is available from the Library of Congress

British Library Cataloguing in Publication Data
A CIP catalogue record for this book is available from the British Library

ISBN 978 1 78592 451 4
eISBN 978 1 78450 828 9

Printed and bound in China

Roxy the Raccoon

A Story to Help Children Learn about Disability and Inclusion

ALICE REEVES

Illustrated by
PHOEBE KIRK

Part of the  Truth & Tails series

Jessica Kingsley Publishers
London and Philadelphia

Roxy the Raccoon lived in the biggest tree in the whole forest.

It was so big that she shared it with some of her best friends.

Roxy lived at
the bottom
of the tree.

Sammy the Squirrel
lived in the middle
of the tree.

Cherry the Chipmunk
lived at the top
of the tree.

The tree grew next to the river, where
Brad the Beaver lived in his dam.

Brad loved to visit Roxy, Sammy, and Cherry in their tree, but Roxy had never been to Brad's dam before.

"Brad, I would love to visit your house," said Roxy one day.

"Why don't you come over tomorrow?" said Brad.

The next day, Roxy made her way
along the river. She was excited
about seeing Brad's house.

When she arrived, she looked up...
and up...and up. The dam was huge!

"Brad, I'm here!" called Roxy.

"Come on up!" said Brad.

"But...I can't get all the way up there with my wheelchair," Roxy said.

"I'm sorry, Roxy," said Brad,
"I didn't think about that."

Roxy was disappointed that she couldn't go to Brad's house, so she went to see what Sammy the Squirrel was doing.

Roxy found Sammy and the other squirrels kicking a ball around.

"Roxy, come and play with us!" called Sammy.

"I'd love to play," said Roxy, "but I can't kick the ball like you squirrels can."

"I'm sorry, Roxy," said Sammy, "I didn't think about that."

Roxy was sad that she couldn't play with Sammy and the other squirrels, so she went home to find Cherry the Chipmunk.

She heard Cherry calling her name from high up in the branches.

"Roxy, come up here," said Cherry. "It's such a beautiful day, I can see the whole forest!"

"I'm sure it's a lovely view," said Roxy, "but there isn't a way for me to get to the top of the tree."

Roxy looked up, feeling upset that she couldn't join her friend.

Just as Roxy was about to go into her house, she heard Brad the Beaver calling her name.

"Roxy!" shouted Brad. "I'm sad you couldn't come to my house. There must be something we can do!"

Roxy thought about it and said, "You could build a ramp for me to wheel my chair up."

"I can do that," said Brad, happily. "Come with me!"

When they arrived at the dam, Brad climbed quickly up to his house.

Roxy heard gnawing and chopping and banging and bashing.

When Brad came back, he had
a long board made of wood.

He pushed it down to where Roxy
was waiting, making a ramp that
led all the way to the top.

"Now you can come to my house any time you want!" said Brad.

Roxy smiled and made her way up the ramp, feeling very happy.

On her way home from Brad's house, Roxy heard Sammy the Squirrel calling her name.

"Roxy!" called Sammy. "I felt sad that you couldn't play with us earlier. Is there a different game we can all play?"

"I like to play catch," said Roxy. "If we play that, then everyone can join in."

"Great idea!" said Sammy.

Roxy and the squirrels had a wonderful time playing catch.

When Roxy and Sammy got home, Brad and Cherry were calling their names from the top of the tree.

"Roxy! Sammy! The sunset is so beautiful tonight, you must come up here and see it!" exclaimed Cherry.

Sammy jumped into the tree,
springing from branch to branch
until he reached the top.

Roxy looked up, sad that she
couldn't see the beautiful sunset.

Then Cherry said, "Roxy, you can come up, too. If we all work together..."

Brad, Cherry, Sammy, and Roxy got to work straight away.

Brad gnawed off long,
bendy branches.

Sammy tied them together
with ivy to make ropes.

Cherry lowered the ropes all the way down to the bottom of the tree, and Roxy tied them tightly around herself.

"Sammy, Brad, Cherry!" called Roxy when she was fastened tight. "Here I come!"

Roxy pulled on the ropes and began to climb up...and up...and up the biggest tree in the forest.

She passed Sammy
the Squirrel's house.

She passed
Cherry the
Chipmunk's house.

Roxy had never been this
far up the tree before!

When Roxy reached the top, she looked down at the forest below and saw animals playing and flowers blooming.

Then Roxy looked up at the sunset, which was bright pink and orange and yellow.

It was a beautiful view.

Roxy turned to look at her three best friends.

"Brad, thank you for building a ramp so that everyone can come to your house," she said.

"It was no trouble," said Brad. "I want you all to come and see me whenever you like."

"Sammy, thank you for changing your game so that we could all play," said Roxy.

"We didn't mind," said Sammy. "It's more fun when everyone can join in."

"Cherry, thank you for helping find a way for me to climb to the top of the tree."

"No problem!" said Cherry. "It's nicer when we can do things together."

After that day, Roxy the Raccoon and her friends worked together to make sure that nobody in the forest ever felt left out again.

Notes for Teachers and Parents

The following open questions can be asked to inspire discussion.

Circle time before reading

★ Have you ever felt left out before?

★ How does it feel to be left out?

★ What does disability mean?

★ What types of disability are there?

★ How can a disability affect people every day?

★ What changes do people with a disability sometimes need in order to get around?

After reading

★ What things do Roxy the Raccoon's friends do to help her?

★ What things do we have around school that would help Roxy? (Walk around and see.)

★ Why does Roxy feel left out at first?

★ How do you think Roxy feels when her friends help her?

★ Why is important to let everyone join in?

★ What can you do in school to make sure no one is left out?

Resources

Scope has a number of resources for early years professionals and primary school teachers: www.scope.org.uk/support/professionals

There is also a Scope community forum for parents and carers of disabled children: https://community.scope.org.uk/categories/carers-of-disabled-children-and-adults

Acknowledgements

Thank you to everyone who helped us to tell Roxy's story, especially Aoife, Nancy, Roger, and Matthew, for your constructive feedback, essential critique, and kind words.

Also in the *Truth & Tails* series

Carlos the Chameleon

A Story to Help Empower Children to Be Themselves

As a chameleon, it's in Carlos's nature to change his colours in order to fit into his surroundings. Carlos is usually green, but can turn pink to join the flamingos, blue to match the frogs, and spotty to resemble the jaguars.

When the other animals find out that Carlos has been changing his colours in order to fit in, they reassure him that his own colour is beautiful and that he doesn't need to change who he is to be accepted and loved by his friends.

Molly the Mole

A Story to Help Children Build Self-Esteem

Molly is a mole with many friends, including a deer, a butterfly, and an owl. Sometimes Molly feels sad because she doesn't look the same as her friends, and feels very different to them. By helping each of them out with a task, Molly learns that her friends love her for the amazing qualities that are unique just to her.

Molly the Mole addresses the difference between the way we perceive ourselves and the way our friends and family perceive us. Molly learns the importance of being kind and patient with others, and that everyone is special in their own way.

Vincent the Vixen

A Story to Help Children Learn about Gender Identity

Vincent is a boy fox who loves to play dress up with their brothers and sisters, but when they always choose to dress up as female characters, Vincent's siblings begin to wonder why.

Vincent comes to realise that they are actually a girl fox, and with the support of friends and family they transition to living as their true self. This is the story of one fox's journey to realising their gender identity and the importance of being who you are.